A Pocket Guide

Hawaiian
ISLANDS

**Text by
U'i Goldsberry, Steven Goldsberry
and Curt Sanburn**

Photography by Douglas Peebles

MUTUAL PUBLISHING

This is an abridged version of the book Beautifull Hawai'i, published in 1998.

Library of Congress Catalog Card Number 2001118591

ISBN-10: 1-56647-499-X
ISBN-13: 978-1-56647-499-3

First Printing, November 2001
Second Printing, March 2004
Third Printing, June 2006
Fourth Printing, April 2008
Fifth Printing, November 2012

Design by Angela Wu-Ki

Mutual Publishing, LLC
1215 Center Street, Suite 210
Honolulu, Hawai'i 96816
Ph (808) 732-1709
Fax (808) 734-4094
Email: info@mutualpublishing.com
www.mutualpublishing.com

Printed in Korea

In late afternoon the Big Island offers a tropical land-scape of rugged lava coastlines and placid waters tinted with the luminous pastels of sunset.

Opposite page: Pu'uhonua o Hōnaunau, the Place of Refuge in the North Kona district, shines as one of the most sacred areas on the Island of Hawai'i. Within its rock boundaries, violators of the *kapu* laws sought sanctuary and purification; and here women, children, the elderly, and the weak found protection during war.

Tables of Contents

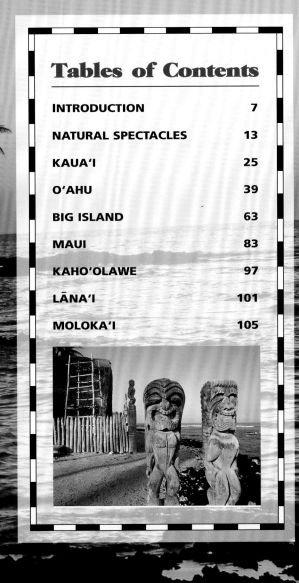

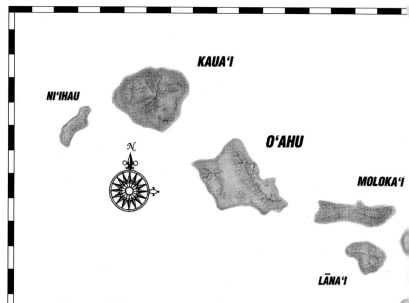

KAUA'I

NI'IHAU

O'AHU

MOLOKA'I

LĀNA'I

THE HAWAIIAN ISLANDS

KAHO'OLAWE

Each of Hawai'i's islands—Kaua'i, O'ahu, Moloka'i, Lāna'i, Maui, Kaho'olawe, the Big Island of Hawai'i—has its own personality.

MAUI

HAWAI'I

Princeville, a resort development near the town of Hanalei on the island of Kaua'i, exudes a tropical tranquillity unrivaled among Hawai'i's hotels. Tiny cove-like beaches of white sand and shimmering aqua-blue water dot the coastline of this, the northernmost tourist destination in Hawai'i.

Introduction

Situated almost dead-center in the middle of the Pacific Ocean, in the relentless surge of wind-tossed waves, lies the most remote landform on earth—the fragmented arc of high islands called Hawai'i. Towering shield volcanoes, now eroded and gullied, comprise the emerald green mountains of this ancient archipelago.

Of the eight major islands, four stand out as the most dramatic and alluring, and not coincidentally the most heavily populated—Kaua'i, O'ahu, Maui, and Hawai'i (The Big Island).

Kaua'i is the oldest of the group at roughly five million years—five or six times as old as Hawai'i, at the opposite end of the chain. Frequent rains (Kaua'i's Mount Wai'ale'ale is the wettest spot on our planet) have eroded the island into broad alluvial plains and deep canyons cut by Hawai'i's only true rivers.

Kaua'i's erosion has had its artistic effect in the forms of steep pinnacles and razorback ridges, remnant mountains draped in velvety folds, gorges whose rock walls reveal millions of years of multi-hued geology, and countless dream-like waterfalls.

Sixty miles to the southeast, across a treacherous channel, lies the island of O'ahu, where Polynesia meets the twenty-first century. Nowhere in Hawai'i are the contemporary realities and complexities of life in paradise more vivid with the booming prosperity, the cultural and racial confluences, the proud history, the trade-offs between preservation and progress played out against a spectacular natural beauty.

The simplest images express it best: Honolulu's glittering high-rises crowded between blue sea and green mountains; freeway traffic cooled by trade winds and gilded by blazing sunsets; the stunning regularity of rainbows arched over the city and its outlying plains.

Honolulu and Waikīkī usually overwhelm any other impression of the island. However, the great surprise to most visitors is how spectacular the rest of O'ahu is, both physically and socially.

Topographically, this 600-square-mile, mature volcanic island is the most varied and intimate of the major Hawaiian Islands. Spread out along O'ahu's four distinct coastlines like a checklist of tropical essentials are coral reefs,

Water from the frequent rains that wash the lush green volcanic peaks of the Hawaiian Islands collect into streams, then cascade in pluming waterfalls to plunge pools. The steep cliffs around the falls drip with a gorgeous display of tropical flora: *kukui*, *lo'ulu* palms, ti, heliconias, gingers, African tulips, and *hala*.

sheltered lagoons, scores of beaches, well-defined bays, view-perfect promontories, mist-shrouded valleys, dry leeward plains, and sheer, fluted cliffs.

Although O'ahu has ultra-famous Waikiki, arguably the best-known island is Maui. Its name is derived from the mischievous Polynesian demigod, Māui, who stole the secret of fire from the gods and slowed the sun's flight across the sky so that Hawaiian days would be longer and warmer.

Like its namesake, the island of Maui revels in the sun and devotes its long days to playful and athletic pleasures. It is the most glamorous and flamboyant of all the Hawaiian Islands. With miles of swimming beaches, two perpetually sunny coasts, awesome mountains, and calm, leeward seaways ringed by a majestic fleet of lesser islands, Maui has every right to its stellar reputation, international charm, and the phrase used to describe it: "Maui no ka 'oi," Maui is the best!

The second youngest and the second largest of the islands, Maui includes in its 728 square miles two distinct volcanic domes—mighty Haleakalā ("House of the Sun") and the compact West Maui Mountains. The two eroded volcanoes are joined by Maui's central isthmus, formed a million years ago when lava from Haleakalā met the shores of West Maui. The isthmus functions as a valley between the peaks.

The island of Hawai'i, commonly called "the Big Island," has only a smattering of man-made environs spread across 4,034 square miles of lava, scrub, and forested mountains. Nature looms large on this island, and nothing else compares.

The Big Island's two major shield volcanoes, Mauna Kea and Mauna Loa, climb almost 14,000 feet above the Pacific. Their wide slopes join the peaks of three smaller volcanoes on the island's perimeter: Kohala, Hualālai, and Kīlauea (the most active one). Northeast trade winds stream across the young landscape, dropping moisture on the windward rain forests, funncling through the saddle areas, accelerating down the leeward declines, and eddying around Mauna Loa's buxom mass.

The Big Island's growth is measured in decades, not millennia. Within the last 200 years, over a hundred eruptions have pushed lava into various precincts across the island's southern half. At times, the molten rivers inundate towns and beaches, and they vanish. New land appears, new little cinder cones, new beaches.

After a century of ranching, fishing, and agriculture, the Big Island has become an international curiosity—the home of an active, drive-in volcano, and mega-hotels built on lava rocks at the edges of idyllic, jewel-like coastlines.

Each island possesses a unique identity, and however you imagine paradise, you're sure to find it just around the bend.

Use this travelogue as an introduction to the treasures of Hawai'i, from its natural spectacles, through its history, to its cherished activities and attractions. Only the highlights are noted here, for busy travelers whose time won't allow for deep exploration. If you want more detailed portraits of Kaua'i, O'ahu, Maui, and the Big Island, refer to the individual island titles in the series.

'Aha'ila i ka pupuhi—Travel with the speed of wind.

The original anthuriums were brought to Hawai'i by an English missionary, Samuel Damon, in 1889 from Colombia, via London. The "Bright Reds" range in size from tiny (peewees) to extra long, and account for almost half of Hawai'i's exotic flower sales.

Liquid lava trickles in luminescent streams over the cooled lava from an older Kīlauea Volcano eruption. The islands of Hawai'i were formed by this "layer upon layer" process of volcanic creation.

Natural Spectacles

Each Hawaiian island vibrates with certain individual energies. Kaua'i, the Garden Isle, whose dormant volcano now erupts with vegetation, glistens with rainwater and the misty spindrift of scouring winter surf. O'ahu, the Gathering Place, is bustling with urban excitement and girdled by more golden beaches than you'll find along any other shore. The Magic Isle, Maui, moves to the pace of ranch-life, resorts, and remote hideaways. And Hawai'i, the Big Island, lives up to its namesake with gigantic, active volcanoes, the most extravagant hotels, and mile upon mile of startlingly unusual scenery.

Created in sequence by a slow, steady northwestward drift of a tectonic plate over a volcanic "hot spot" deep in the Pacific, these islands display astounding differences of geology and landscape, structure and grace. The process that created this archipelago began 70 million years ago with the creation of what is now the Meiji Seamount, and continues today on the Big Island at the southeastern end.

The typical young landform of the Hawaiian Islands is a rounded "shield" volcano, built by innumerable thin lava flows. Mauna Loa on the Big Island is a classic—and still active—shield volcano, rising gently to its 13,800-foot height above the crashing waves of the Pacific.

On the major islands it's easy to see the geological evolution from the swelling shapes of intact young shield volcanoes on the Big Island and Maui to the heavily eroded, jagged topography of Kaua'i. Islands to the north shrink steadily from oceanic rocks to atolls, and beyond the last dry land of Kure Atoll there are hundreds of miles of seamounts leading at last to Meiji, the first island of this ancient chain.

As you tour the Islands, and peruse these pages, take a moment to imagine the geological history of the images before you, how stubborn sea cliffs were once a molten flow of dense basalt, how a plain has been created over centuries of stream runoff and intermittent waterfalls have grooved a precipice, how reefs have bloomed over wave-cooled lava, and how a cinder cone crater has collapsed to form a bay. Like no other such limited geographical area, Hawai'i displays the phoenix power of the earth's unending cycles of change.

A golden path of fading sunlight bestows its blessing of romance on a tropical paradise. Such soothing displays of idyllic beauty contrast the jagged coastlines, volcanic peaks, and raw, elemental forces of the Hawaiian Islands.

Keʻē cliff, just west of Hāʻena on the island of Kauaʻi, is closely connected to the Pele legends. After Lohiʻau died of love for Pele, his body was sequestered in a cave on this cliff. Hiʻiaka and her companion, Wahine-omaʻo (green woman), climbed the cliff and, with herbs and long prayers, Hiʻiaka restored Lohiʻau to life. Three rainbows appeared, and the legendary characters slid down the rainbows to earth.

Chinaman's Hat (Mokoliʻi) floats between a
tranquil sea and morning sky ablaze with
orange, deep purple, pink, and lavender light.
Such days of calm clarity are rare on the windward coast of Oʻahu: almost the entire southern
half of the Koʻolau range stretches as far as the
eye can see. The mountains are usually shroud-
ed in rain clouds. Looking toward Heʻeia, this
angle of Mokoliʻi Island argues strongly for its
modern name—Chinaman's Hat.

It's hard to see why on this calm afternoon, but when wave swells hit this coast, Makapu'u Beach becomes one of the premier bodysurfing spots on O'ahu. The rough currents of the Kaiwi Channel between O'ahu and Moloka'i wrap around Makapu'u cliff, creating ideal conditions for wave riding.

A shroud of misty clouds drifts through the rain forests in Hawai'i Volcanoes National Park. Black-barked 'ōhi'a trees tower over a blanket of *hāpu'u* and *'ama'u* ferns that cover the forest floor.

The lacey fronds of the *hāpu'u*, or tree fern, form the low canopy of ground cover in the rain forests of the Hawai'i Volcanoes National Park. Their shade holds the moisture close to the rocky soil, allowing splendid mosses to grow.

The beauty of Lumaha'i Beach, near Hanalei on the island of Kaua'i, was called Nurses' Beach in the 1958 movie musical, *South Pacific*. Breadfruit trees that once lined the shore were said to have been planted by a *menehune* named Weli.

KAUA'I

FACTS AND FIGURES

County: Kaua'i; includes islands of Kaua'i and
   Ni'ihau
County seat: Līhu'e
Land area: Kaua'i, 552.3 square miles; Ni'ihau,
   69.5 square miles
Population: 58,303 (2000); Ni'ihau, 160 (2000)
Highest point: Kawaikini, 5,243 feet; Ni'ihau,
   1,250 feet
Shoreline: 90 miles; Ni'ihau, 45 miles
Extreme length and width:
   33 miles by 25 miles
Average annual temperature:
   Lihu'e: 79.95°F
Highest recorded temperature: 95°F
Lowest recorded temperature:
   Sea level: 50°F
   Koke'e (elevation 3,600): 29°F
Average annual rainfall:
   Po'ipū, 34.35 inches
   Wai'ale'ale summit, 444 inches
Hotel and condominium rental units: approxi-
   mately 8,002 (2006)
Visitors per year: approximately 1,270,013 (2006)
State parks: 10; County parks: 67

The sharply furrowed mountains of the Napali Coast, eroded by the pounding rains that frequent this island, stand as natural ramparts protecting the inland areas of Kaua'i. Campers are required to obtain permits before making the long, switch-back hike along the coast to the campsites in this state park and forest reserve.

KAUAʻI

auaʻi stands to this day as a place apart. On most days, the 60-mile Kaʻieʻiewaho or Kauaʻi Channel is wide enough that Kauaʻi and its nearest neighbor, Oʻahu, are out of sight of each other. Canoe paddlers in ancient days had to know their course between these islands because often at mid-channel neither island is visible. Kauaʻi remained independent for 15 years after Kamehameha the Great in 1795 completed his conquests of the Big Island, Maui, Molokaʻi, Lānaʻi, and Oʻahu.

Archaeologists have found on Kauaʻi mysterious stone work and implements never seen on the other Hawaiian Islands. Ancient Kauaʻi and neighboring Niʻihau had their own dialect of the Hawaiian language, using "t" and "r" in words where the windward islanders used "k" and "l." More than any other island, Kauaʻi is steeped in lively storytelling, legends, and myths. Every rock, peak, and cave has ancient significance; gods and ghosts animate the remote beaches.

Kauaʻi is the oldest Hawaiian island at roughly five million years of age, five or six times as old as Hawaiʻi, the tallest and youngest of the islands, at the other end of the island chain. Heavy rains delivered by the northeast trade winds have eroded the island. Its alluvial plains are thick and rich, and its river valleys cut deep into the heart of the circular island's volcanic core.

The ancient Hawaiians may have been aware that their island would someday disappear. Legend says that a rock pinnacle at Hāʻena on Kauaʻi's north shore will stand as long as Kauaʻi does. When the rock falls, the island will crumble. This is the succession of geological events for Hawaiian islands: first an island, then a rock, then an atoll, and finally a shoal, of concern only to ships' navigators.

But Kauaʻi's erosion has its positive side effects. One of Kauaʻi's chief attractions is the drama of the wind- and water-carved landscape. Deep iron-hued canyons, tall pinnacles and dragon-teeth ridges, breathtaking sea cliffs spilling waterfalls, corrugated mountainsides like green drapery hung from the cloudy heavens—these are Kauaʻi's treasures.

Mount Wai'ale'ale, the second highest peak on Kaua'i (5,080 feet), has an average rainfall of over 476 inches. Its Hawaiian name is quite appropriate. Wai'ale'ale means "rippling water or overflowing."

When the British explorer Captain James Cook landed at Waimea in January 1778, the taro farmers and fishermen of west Kaua'i thought his ships were floating islands covered with tall trees. They flung themselves to the ground when he or his men approached. They gave him water, pigs, bananas, yams, and fish—everything he wanted. In Waimea Valley, Cook noted the neat geometry of the fields and the complex irrigation system. Expedition artist John Webber sketched the native *heiau* (temples) with their stone platforms, wooden towers, and grimacing idols.

Across the island at Wailua, the island's *ali'i* (chiefs) and *kāhuna* (priests) knew nothing of the momentous events in Waimea. They carried on as usual. They gathered taxes of food from the *maka'āinana* (commoners), feasted, played games, surfed, punished *kapu* (law) violators, had children, and managed their vast estates. Their history was preserved in hours-long chants memorized by skilled court chanters who freely mixed history, legend, and fantasy.

Hanalei means "crescent" in Hawaiian. This bay is the largest on Kaua'i, the scene of yacht racing during the summer and world-class surfing in the winter.

Limahuli Gardens, on 1,000 acres in Limahuli Valley, is a lush sanctuary for many rare and native Hawaiian plant species, as well as introduced tropicals that love the very wet conditions.

The 52-foot Kīlauea Lighthouse, built in 1913, once guided ships from the Orient past Kaua'i and on to O'ahu. Poised 200 feet above the Pacific on the tip of the Kilauea Peninsula, this weathered old beacon no longer flashes.

Opposite page: Following a heavy rain, two or three main streams cascade down the 80-foot drop of Wailua Falls.

Sun-tinged clouds, golden sand, ancient palms—a secret beach on Kaua'i.

The chants told stories of giant warriors and petulant goddesses, of great ancestors and of creation itself (as in the famed creation chant called the *Kumulipo*); stories of voyages to and from Tahiti and the Marquesas Islands; and marvelous tales of the *menehune*, a legendary race of spry mountain people who built huge walls, ditches, *heiau*, and fishponds in the dark of night.

Anthropologists now say that there is no evidence that the *menehune* ever really existed. The legend, they believe, recalls the earliest Marquesan settlers on Kaua'i who were subsequently ruled by the later-arriving Tahitians. The scientists have yet to explain adequately the unique "menehune" stonework and engineering feats of ancient Kaua'i.

The legends remind everyone that there is more to Kaua'i's landscape than erosion. Stones are still piled in simple terraces where gods once

danced. A sleeping giant dreams on a hilltop, while below him, in Kapaʻa, families shop for frozen food. At Haʻena, two stones are thought to be two legendary brothers who came ashore to die after a long sea voyage. Their sister is a rock out on the reef, visible at low tide.

Though its erosion continues unabated, Kauaʻi remains a vibrant, formidable island. It urges you to listen to its stories and understand its past. In doing so, it asks you to protect its future so that the life of the island, the murmuring mysteries of its ancient valleys and cloud-shrouded mountains, will never erode.

A traveler wrote 50 years ago: ". . . most of all, Kauaʻi remains in my memory an island of fable, so near its own myths that they materialize out of its rocks and hills and live in its shifting light."

Waimea Canyon, known as the Grand Canyon of the Pacific, is a 3,600-foot-deep chasm carved by Waimea River and Kaua'i's frequent torrential rains.

To hike the Nāpali Coast you must follow the narrow, winding, switch-backs of the Kalalau Trail.

An endangered Hawaiian Green Sea Turtle rides a wave surge over the reefs off Kaua'i's southern coast.

It is still possible to take late afternoon runs along the secluded beaches at Princeville.

The beach at Po'ipū was a sunny haven for ancient Hawaiian chiefs and today is a popular resort destination.

During the summer, when the water off the Nā Pali Coast is placid and blue, Spinner and Bottlenose dolphins race and weave in front of kayaks and tour boats.

The lacy, green canopy of the Fern Grotto, at the head of the Wailua River and just south of Wailua Falls, is a favorite spot for romantic tropical weddings.

This panoramic view of the windward coast of O'ahu from Kāne'ohe to Kualoa shows the classic fluted ridges and dramatic pinnacles of the Ko'olau mountain range.

O'AHU

FACTS AND FIGURES

County: City and County of Honolulu

Land area: 596.7 square miles

Population: 876,151 (2000)

Highest point: Mt. Ka'ala, 4,003 feet

Shoreline: 112 miles

Extreme length and width:
    44 miles by 30 miles

Average annual temperature: 77.4°F

Highest recorded temperature: 99°F

Lowest recorded temperature: 42°F

Average annual rainfall at Honolulu
    Airport: 22.13 inches

Average annual rainfall:
    Mānoa Valley, 168.63 inches

Hotel and condominium rental units:
    34,008 (2006)

Visitors per year: 4,727,496 (2006)

State parks: 32

County parks: 282

The coastline from Ala Moana to Waikīkī. The three stretches of white sand are Ala Moana Beach (bottom), Magic Island (center), and Waikīkī. The long, flat concrete slab to the left is the Ala Moana Shopping Center, once the largest shopping mall in the United States. The Ala Wai Yacht Harbor marks the entrance to Waikīkī, and the green oasis in the middle of towering highrises is the Ala Wai Municipal Golf Course.

O'AHU

Welcome to the island of O'ahu, the urban stronghold of Hawai'i's far-flung island kingdom. With a population just cresting one million, O'ahu supports nearly 80 percent of the state's residents, and entertains more tourists than all the other islands combined. But, while the sprawling metropolis of modern Honolulu/Waikīkī reaches skyward with its concrete and steel high-rises, the stunning natural beauties of the island remain, from the rain-catching green of the Ko'olau Mountains behind the city to the remote beaches, bays, and windswept points in "the country."

O'ahu is a wealth of contrasts. There are jammed freeways (with five cars for every six people, the island endures the most automobile-dense society on earth), but also there are rainbows rising through the valley mists beyond the traffic. Neighborhoods, as distinct and varied as the races living there, are linked by O'ahu's busy roads. Many old-time Japanese families have settled in Mō'ili'ili and Kaimukī, the Caucasians east of Diamond Head, Filipinos and Samoans in Kalihi, the Chinese in Chinatown. There is much ethnic and class mixing, however. A Buddhist temple sits a block away from a Mexican restaurant. A Japanese language school shares a building with a Portuguese bakery.

And the roads take you out of Honolulu's 25-mile long urban corridor on the South Shore into the farms and plantations in the verdant heart of the island, and on to the North Shore and its wilderness of waves and rugged coast. In twenty minutes the complications of the big-city rush give way to the serenity of sun and surf.

The long Ko'olau mountain range to the east and the Wai'anae range to the west, with a broad central plain in between, define the island. The 4,000-foot peaks, sloping ridges and steep-walled *pali* (cliffs) are the remains of the much higher Ko'olau and Wai'anae volcanoes that emerged from the Pacific about three million years ago. On O'ahu, nature has had plenty of time to rearrange its crude volcanoes into a magical landscape. Eons of stream and wave erosion have carried much of the original mass back into

Surfers at Waimea Bay race the cresting power of the North Shore's winter surf. Riding the mountainous waves of Waimea Bay is the ultimate test of a waterman's courage, and the greatest thrill in sports.

the sea, leaving behind the soft, deeply folded draperies of Windward O'ahu and the alternating valleys and ridges that provide Honolulu's dramatic backdrop. Later volcanic activity added the finishing touch with a series of volcanic cones: the beloved landmarks of Diamond Head, Punchbowl, and Koko Head.

O'ahu has been known as "the gathering place" since ancient days, when chiefs from the other, more populous islands conferred at Waikīkī, which was then neutral ground.

O'ahu's modern history begins in late 1794, 16 years after British Captain James Cook found and named the Sandwich Islands, when a British fur trading ship, *Jackal*, inched through a break in the coral reef protecting a small O'ahu fishing village called Kou and found a commodious harbor that the sailors named Fair Haven—"Honolulu" in Hawaiian. The promise of a safe anchorage and nearby fresh water and food (and, no

Hanauma Bay was formed when the seaward wall of an ancient volcano crater collapsed. Aptly named, *hanauma* means "curved bay."

doubt, its exotic name) drew adventurers, sandalwood traders, merchants, and whalers from America and Europe to Honolulu. New England Protestant missionaries quickly followed—to remind the sailors away from home of their spiritual responsibilities, and to clothe and convert the Hawaiians. By 1850, when King Kamehameha III relocated the royal capital here from Lahaina, Maui, Honolulu was a bustling Pacific port-of-call.

As the city grew, its wealthy residents sought refuge from the dust, heat, and overdressed fussiness of Victorian Honolulu. They found it two miles away at Waikīkī, a traditional surfing and fishing beach reserved for Oʻahu's *aliʻi*. Hawaiʻi's royalty built modest cottages there, in the ancient coconut groves at Helumoa, where the Royal Hawaiian Hotel now stands. Western businessmen followed and soon learned from the Hawaiians how to surf the gentle waves. In 1901, the Moana—a large modern hotel that rose higher than the coconut palms—opened with 100 visiting Shriners as its first guests.

The Polynesian Cultural Center in the small windward town of La'ie is staffed by Polynesian and mainland U.S. students attending Brigham Young University-Hawai'i campus.

Hula dancers at Waimea Falls Park provide daily cultural education and demonstrations of Hawaiian dance and martial arts.

Honolulu is the state capital, by far its largest city, and the headquarters for banking, construction, transportation, agriculture, manufacturing, and tourism. The U.S. Army, Navy, and Air Force commands based on O'ahu involve more than 116,000 military personnel and their dependents, and control one quarter of O'ahu's land area.

The City and County of Honolulu—a single political entity—covers the entire island; "Honolulu" usually refers to the urban swath along O'ahu's south shore from Koko Head in the east to Pearl Harbor in the west, and from the ocean into the Ko'olau Mountains. Having their own distinct personalities are the bedroom communities of Kailua and Kāne'ohe on the far side of the Ko'olau mountains; the sprawling commuter suburbs of 'Aiea, Pearl City, Waipahu, 'Ewa, and Mililani to the west; the military centers at Pearl Harbor, Hickam Air Force Base, Kāne'ohe Marine Corps Base Headquarters, Wheeler Air Force Base, and the U.S. Army Schofield Barracks; and the rural coastal communities of Wai'anae, Waialua, Hale'iwa, Kahuku, Lā'ie, Kahalu'u and Waimānalo.

Slightly more than half of the people on O'ahu were born in Hawai'i and call themselves *kama'āina*, children of the land. The rest, *malihini*, moved here. Thirty-three percent of the total population is Caucasian or *haole*. Another 21 percent is first-, second-, third-, or fourth-generation Japanese: *issei, nisei, sansei,* or *yonsei*. Hawaiians or part-Hawaiians constitute 18 percent. The remaining 28 percent includes Filipinos, Chinese, Portuguese, Samoans, Koreans, Tongans, Vietnamese, Cambodians, African Americans, and Puerto Ricans, in that order of significance. Nearly half of O'ahu's marriages are interracial.

This colorblindness, this hospitality, is the legacy of the Hawaiian people. From the moment of first contact with Europeans in 1778, the Hawaiians were open-armed. Tragically, the cost of aloha was devastating, as introduced diseases, economic exploitation, and political conquest brought the Hawaiians to the edge of extinction.

Somehow the spirit of aloha prevailed, and the Hawaiian host-culture is still the touchstone for almost every aspect of Hawai'i's uniqueness: the racial harmony, graceful way of life, famous music and dance, colorful integration of nature into man-made things, and stewardship of the *'āina*, the land.

Despite intensive land and golf developments, O'ahu's pleasures are the same today as yesterday. The trade winds continue to blow and the pure

The pyramidal peak of Puʻuʻōhulehule looks down upon Kualoa Regional Park and Hōkūleʻa Beach, the site of many landings of ancient voyaging canoes.

A glimpse of the sparkling skyline of Honolulu's high-rises beyond the grooved green of the Ko'olau Mountains.

colors of the mountains and the sea continue to amaze. Honolulu is still, by any measure, a glamorous, glorious city. Every day its golden people prove the remarkable durability of the aloha spirit, that guileless local friendliness that transcends the realities of the late twentieth century.

Towering above the central plains of Oʻahu, and stretching from Kaʻena Point to ʻEwa, the Waiʻanae Mountains are what remains of the older of two volcanoes that created the island. Kolekole Pass, the hallow declivity in this range, marks what some believe to be the flight path Japanese "zeros" used in their attack on Pearl Harbor.

Sunset gold silhouettes the coconut palms at Ala Moana Beach Park.

The light of early morning glints over the foot of Diamond Head as another glorious day in paradise begins.

The USS *Arizona* Memorial shrine straddles the ghostly hulk of the USS *Arizona*.

Lanikai Beach, one of the highest-priced neighborhoods on the windward coast, is known for
its two offshore islands, the Mokuluas. Once an
ancient fishing spot, this mile-long bay of calm
water is great for swimming and kayaking.

'Iolani Palace was built in 1882 by King David Kalākaua and Queen Kapi'olani during the twilight years of the Hawaiian monarchy.

Colorful spinnakers plume as the weekly Friday yacht races begin from the entrance to the Ala Wai Yacht Harbor.

The colors of the sea at Kailua Beach Park are as extraordinary as the quality of the fine golden sand.

The gentle breezes and lake-flat waters of Kailua Beach are perfect for outrigger canoe

The Nu'uanu Pali Lookout affords a very convenient view of the corrugated ridges of the Ko'olau Mountains.

Once a wonderland of coral gardens, Kāne'ohe Bay is making a strong comeback from siltation due to overdevelopment.

The Pleasant Hawaiian Hula Show, once known as the Kodak Hula Show, is an exhibition of classical Hawaiian and Polynesian music and dance performed every week on Tuesday, Wednesday, and Thursday mornings at 10:00 am at the Waikiki Shell.

The Ala Wai Yacht Harbor, at the mouth of the Ala Wai Canal, provides mooring for pleasure craft from around the world.

The upper floors of the Sheraton Waikiki Hotel offer this view of Diamond Head and the white, crescent beach of Waikīkī.

During the summer months, the sun sets into the water off Waikīkī Beach.

Hawai'i's young women of every nationality train and participate in hula demonstrations and celebrations like the Aloha Festival.

Kūkā'ilimoku, Kamehameha the Great's war god, is exhibited in a sealed glass case at the Bishop Museum main gallery.

The classic harbor landmark, Aloha Tower, greeted seafaring visitors and merchants coming to Honolulu. Today, the newly renovated Aloha Tower hosts an upscale marketplace.

Serving the best Chinese food to Honolulu residents since 1882, Wo Fat's Chop Suey Restaurant in Chinatown is an important historical, cultural, and sentimental landmark.

Hawaiian masons cut 14,000 large coral blocks to build Kawaiahaʻo Congregational Church between 1830 and 1840.

Punchbowl Crater, once known as Pūowaina, or "the hill of placing (sacrifices)," today serves as the home of the National Memorial Cemetery of the Pacific.

A 45-minute jeep ride over unimproved roads transports visitors from the tropical scenery of the Saddle Road to the high-mountain snows of Mauna Kea. The summit of this great mountain offers the remarkably thin, clear air that astronomers find ideal for star-gazing.

BIG ISLAND

FACTS AND FIGURES

County: Hawai'i

County seat: Hilo

Land area: 4,028 square miles

Population: 148,677 (2000)

Highest point:
  Mauna Kea summit, 13,796 feet

Shoreline: 266 miles

Extreme length and width:
  93 miles by 76 miles

Average annual temperature, Hilo: 74.3°F

Highest recorded temperature: 95°F

Lowest recorded temperature,
  at sea level: 50°F;
  at Mauna Kea's summit: 11°F

Average annual rainfall,
  at Kawaihae: 9.09 inches;
  Hilo Airport: 126.39 inches

Hotel and condominium rental units:
  11,247 (2006)

Visitors per year: 1,687,986 (2006)

State parks: 19

County parks: 126

Just outside of Hilo, 'Akaka Falls drops 442 feet straight down. Protected and cared for by the Hawai'i State Park service, this cascade and plunge pool are surrounded by a rain forest of giant ginger, heliconia, ferns, orchids, and bamboo.

BIG ISLAND

The island of Hawai'i, commonly called "the Big Island," by locals is the youngest, broadest, and highest island in the chain. The expanse and sheer magnitude of this geologically alive landmass make every human structure—including the glitzy mega-resorts along the western shore—seem paltry by comparison.

The island comprises five shield volcanoes: Kohala, the oldest and most eroded; Hualālai; Mauna Kea, the highest; and the two active ones—mighty Mauna Loa, and its little sister Kīlauea, which has been erupting for over 14 years. Mauna Kea, if measured from its base on the ocean floor, is the tallest mountain in the world. These capacious peaks support varied landscapes, from parched black lava deserts to highland scrub to dense rain forests and alpine cloud forests.

During Hawai'i's recorded history (the last two centuries) more than a hundred major eruptions have reshaped the southern districts of the island, especially in Puna. The lava is part of the nonstop process that began a million years ago and that still builds the island. Rivers of molten rock burn towns, inundate the foundations, and leave behind only fresh fields of black stone. Beaches turn to cliffs and instant new beaches of surf-blown lava particles appear. A fire fountain deposits a new cinder cone. Earthquakes drop sections of coastline a foot or two. Roads close.

The Big Island shivers with life. A dynamic energy animates the whole landscape, whether it's actually bubbling with magma or not. It's hard to describe this living land adequately. It has to be felt.

Until recently the island enjoyed a sleepy anonymity, its economy based on sugar cane and ranching. Then the big resorts began sprouting up along the perpetually sunny leeward coast, the Kona airport expanded, and the volcanic wonderland became an international destination. Its quiet little towns have started to fuss about traffic lights. Suddenly it seems

The broad, snowcapped dome of Mauna Kea, the "white mountain," towers over the heart of *paniolo* country.

that the entire world is driving past the tiny post office, flashing cameras, and squinting at road maps.

Yet the new grand hotels, airports, roads, shopping centers, and warehouse districts are still dwarfed by all the outdoor grandeur. The overwhelming scale of the island—and the power it suggests—render everything else insignificant.

The Hawaiians understood this. Remnants of their life as it was before the *haole* (foreigners; Caucasians) arrived are rather insubstantial: just a few trails, agricultural terraces, fishponds, walls, rock carvings (petroglyphs), shelter sites, and several large platforms of rock, called *heiau*. These stony ramparts were built atop hills or at strategic harbors or on advantageous fields. *Heiau* were places of worship and ritual, dedicated to fishing gods, gods of the fields, the great lizard gods (*mo'o*), war gods, and the ancestral gods of the great chiefs. Men, gods, and nature met at the stone altars to honor the sacred compacts which bound them inextricably and fearfully together. Those who study the history and culture of the Hawaiians invariably note the remarkable harmony with nature sustained by these muscular Polynesians, who used their unsurpassed seafaring arts to find Paradise.

They first landed at South Point, Ka Lae, on the Big Island about 1,500

Helmeted cyclists on bike tours are a common sight along the roads of the Kohala Coast.

years ago. Westerners, or what the Hawaiians politely called *haole*, arrived in 1778, when Captain James Cook of His Majesty's Navy discovered Kaua'i. A year later Cook's ships returned, anchoring at Kealakekua Bay, a few miles south of today's Kailua-Kona. The British captain was royally feted; but later he was clubbed to death in a scuffle, when some Hawaiians stole a ship's launch and caused a confrontation. A shooting incident followed. To shield themselves from British bullets, the Hawaiian villagers held up flimsy mats woven from the leaves of the *hala* tree.

One young chief who watched the brief barrage was Kamehameha, the Lonely One, who would later conquer the Big Island, Maui, and O'ahu with the help of *haole* guns. He established the Kamehameha dynasty and the Kingdom of Hawai'i, which lasted over 100 years.

New England missionaries arrived at Kailua-Kona in 1819. Eight short decades later the Hawaiian Islands were annexed by the United States. During the intervening years, the Hawaiian population, ravaged by introduced diseases, declined from at least 300,000 to about 50,000.

By the time of annexation, the lands of Hawai'i had already shifted to private ownership and had been consolidated in huge *haole*-owned cattle ranches and sugar plantations. A small cattle herd left in Kohala by English captain George Vancouver as a gift for the chief Kamehameha became the nucleus for what is now the Parker Ranch and its impressive 225,000 acres of ranch land and 55,000 head of cattle.

The sugar plantation managers of the Hāmākua and Kaʻū districts, in need of cheap and dependable labor, arranged for the immigration of foreign workers into Hawaiʻi to tend and harvest the profitable sugar fields. First, laborers came from China, then Portugal, Japan, Korea, Okinawa, and, finally, the Philippines. They did the backbreaking work, fulfilled their contracts, saved money, started families, and eventually moved from the plantation camps into towns or to Oʻahu.

Coffee groves in Kona, lettuce fields in Kamuela, macadamia orchards in Kaʻū, and cow pastures in Kohala give the Big Island relief from the endless plantation "lawns" that characterize the other islands. Diversified agriculture has allowed each of the island's far-flung rural communities to develop its own unique character.

Hilo, the Big Island's big town, had the airport, seaport, and easy access to Kīlauea volcano, which had been set aside by the U.S. government in 1916 as Volcanoes National Park. Hilo was the logical place for an infant sightseeing industry, and a few hotels were built there in the early 1960s. But the rainy climate kept the visitor counts low, while Oʻahu and Maui's visitor industries boomed.

The old royal playground at Kona, on the drier leeward coast, had blue sky and history to give this area prestige. By the early 1970s, its sunny coastline was busy with low-rise condos, hotels, and pricey vacation homes. Keāhole Airport near Kona began accepting flights direct from the mainland.

The big ranches sold huge oceanfront lava fields in South Kohala and North Kona to developers from the mainland and Japan, whose ambitions and financial resources were bigger than anything Hawaiʻi had ever seen. The resort boom was on.

One landowner who didn't have to sell was Bishop Estate, the feeholder to hundreds of thousands of acres on Hawaiʻi, Maui, and Oʻahu. Hawaiʻi's largest private landholder, Bishop Estate is the legacy of the Kamehameha dynasty, held in perpetual trust for the education and general benefit of Hawaiian children. It has developed a multi-hotel golf resort at Keauhou on lands where the warrior-king Kamehameha I once lived.

It is not certain when Kamehameha was born, because dates were not

Mo'okini Heiau, in North Kohala, was constructed around A.D. 480. The grass hut housed the *kahu*, or caretaker of the *heiau*.

Lapakahi is a partially restored Hawaiian fishing village dating back to the fourteenth century. Paths, low rock walls of the old dwellings, and specimen trees and plants used by the Hawaiians are the only signs of a vanished way of life.

accurately kept by the Hawaiian oral historians. Scholars assume it was in the 1750s, in Kohala at ʻUpolu Point, where the supposed birthing site has been sensitively preserved.

As a boy, Kamehameha learned modern warfare and modern commerce and took advantage of both. He forged the Hawaiian nation from a group of warring chiefdoms and made it prosperous according to the European definition of prosperity. When he died in Kona in 1819 at his compound at Kailua Bay, where the King Kamehameha Hotel now stands, he was an old man still praying to his gods.

The life and legend of Kamehameha pervade the Big Island even today. The touchstones of the island's history and lore are his birthplace at ʻUpolu Point, his great war *heiau* at Puʻukoholā, his lands at Keauhou, the fishponds at ʻAnaehoʻomalu, his refuge at Waipiʻo, and the site of his death on the shores of Kailua Bay. After his passing, Kamehameha's sacred bones, thought to be the vessels for his immortal spirit, were carried away to a secret burial cave. Although many fortune hunters have searched for this greatest tomb of Hawaiʻi's royalty, the cave has never been found.

Kaunaʻoa Beach, within the Mauna Kea Beach Resort in South Kohala, lies about a mile south of Kawaihae on Queen Kaʻahumanu Highway.

The reconstructed *heiau* and Hale o Keawe mausoleum at Puʻuhonua o Hōnaunau (Place of Refuge) stand as monuments to the complex social structure that governed the lives of the ancient Hawaiians.

The coarse, icy snow of Mauna Kea is a challenge for even the most expert snowman artist. This man, made with the rarely used "pack and slap" technique, won't last long in the tropical sun, even at these elevations.

A lonely *paniolo* from Kamuela heads home through the green hills and fertile pastures of Parker Ranch, the largest cattle ranch in America.

The calm waters of Reed's Bay in Hilo, one of the most expansive natural harbors in Hawai'i, make it very popular with yachting enthusiasts.

Named for the constant iridescence that appears in the sunlit cascading water, Rainbow Falls feeds the Wailuku River just outside of Hilo.

Lili'uokalani Garden, a Japanese-style park complete with ponds, pagodas, and bridges, is the largest formal Oriental garden outside of Japan.

This hanging red jade vine is just one of the many rare and exotic specimens of flora found at the Nani Mau Botanical Gardens.

73

The gullied terrain of the Hāmākua Coast, north of Hilo, was once covered with fields of sugar cane. Now the rolling plains and sheer ravines are known as "the macadamia nut capital of Hawai'i."

Hiking clearly marked trails through the rain forests of the Hawai'i Volcanoes National Park is a wonderful way to see tree ferns and 'ōhi'a.

Like a scene of pre-historic majesty, the dramatic coastline near Pololū in North Kohala has the rugged power of new earth.

Fiery orange and ash black in summer, the cinder cones at the summit of Mauna Kea soften in winter beneath white blankets of pure, high-altitude snow.

The black sands at Punalu'u Beach in the South Point district are the result of Pele's mad rush to the sea.

The magnificently clear waters of Kealakekua Bay are perfect for viewing the young reefs that have formed over submerged lava flows.

This view into a lava tube through a collapsed "skylight" shows a river of 2,000-degree lava.

Fire and water collide in dramatic roars, hisses, and plumes of smoke as Pele, the volcano goddess, pushes new land into the sea.

The southeastern flank of Kīlauea Volcano erupted on January 3, 1983, with spectacular lava fountains shooting into the sky. Though not always so dramatic, the current phase of volcanic activity has lasted over 14 years.

The rugged Puna Coast, still raw with young lava, simmers in the golden light of the setting sun.

Rivulets of gleaming lava converge on their journey from Kīlauea Volcano to the sea.

Pleasure yachts and commercial sightseeing vessels dot the deep blue waters off the historic town of Lahaina. Located on the western coast of the island of Maui, this quaint little town, now a renowned tourist destination, once boiled with excitement as the center of the whaling industry of the Pacific.

MAUI

FACTS AND FIGURES

County: Maui, which includes the
   islands of Maui, Moloka'i, Lāna'i,
   and Kaho'olawe
County seat: Wailuku
Land area: 727.2 square miles
Population: 117,644 (2000)
   Includes Lanai and Moloka'i
Highest point: Pu'u'ula'ula (Red Hill),
   Haleakalā, 10,023 feet
Shoreline: 120 miles
Extreme length and width:
   48 miles by 26 miles
Average annual temperature: 75.55°F
Highest recorded temperature: 98°F
Lowest recorded temperature
   (at sea level): 48°F; at Haleakalā's
   summit: 14°F
Average annual rainfall: Kīhei, 15.2
   inches
Average annual rainfall: Pu'u Kukui,
   West Maui Mountains, 300 plus inches
Hotel and condominium rental units:
   18,441 (2006)
Visitors per year: 2,516,215 (2006)
State parks: 8

A line of cupped cinder cones crosses the desolate interior of Haleakalā Valley. Many have compared this barren view to the surface of the moon. At sunrise, the sun god Lā puts on a spectacular show for those adventurous souls who brave the cold and pre-dawn darkness.

MAUI

The island of Maui gets its name from the muscular Polynesian trickster Maui the demigod, who is credited in legend with fishing up the entire chain of the Hawaiian Islands with a magical fish hook. He also climbed to the top of the island's mighty volcano—Haleakalā, the "House of the Sun"—and pushed the sky high into the heavens so people could walk upright, and run and jump without fear of knocking their heads on the sky god's belly.

That mythical dynamism is central to the island that bears Maui's name, and plays itself out daily in the robust activities of residents and tourists alike. A certain freedom pervades the magical atmosphere of this high-sky place, and everyone revels in its unmatched venues for windsurfing, mountain hiking, snorkeling, cycling, sailing, and plain lying out in the Maui sunshine.

The second largest of the Islands, Maui is dominated by Haleakalā, rising 10,023 feet above sea level, and the older West Maui Mountains, at a maximum height of 5,778 feet at the top of Pu'u Kukui. The isthmus between the two volcanic peaks supports most of Maui's growing population and its waning sugar cane industry. The county seat, Wailuku, on the northern end of the isthmus, is joined by its sister town Kahului, site of the island's deep-water port and an airport that accepts direct flights from the U.S. mainland.

Offshore are four junior islands, all part of Maui County. Sleepy Moloka'i struggles to maintain its rural character. Lāna'i was recently transformed from a pineapple plantation to an exclusive private resort. Kaho'olawe was a U.S. Navy bombing target for many years. And Molokini, a tiny crescent-shaped volcanic cone, is very popular as a snorkeling destination.

Together with the Big Island of Hawai'i, Maui was the stage for ancient Hawai'i's most important events and wars. An era of peace between the rival chiefs of Maui and Hawai'i gave way in the 1600s to

The winding switchbacks and hairpin curves on the road to Hāna have helped maintain the area's quaint ambiance. Many a traveler has lost a breakfast or lunch alongside this swerving, turning byway.

two centuries of endless bloodshed. The Maui dynasty of Kekaulike and his son Kahekili was finally defeated in 1790 by the powerful chief from the Big Island, Kamehameha the Conqueror.

By 1802, Kamehameha had unified all of the Hawaiian Islands except Kaua'i (which he obtained peacefully in 1810). As the first king of a united Hawai'i, he established his royal capital at Lahaina on Maui's leeward coast.

To show his respect for the superior Maui bloodlines, and to secure those bloodlines for his royal heirs, Kamehameha married two of Maui's most chiefly women: Ka'ahumanu, and the sacred princess Ke'opuolani. After his death, his Maui queens retired the old Hawaiian gods and, at the urging of their Protestant missionary advisors, led the Hawaiian conversion to Christianity. *Heiau*, the simple stone temples of Hawaiian worship, were torn down and replaced by churches and schools, where texts printed in the Hawaiian language taught spiritual and practical learning.

South of Hāna, near the end of the paved road, are the Pools of 'Ohe'o. A series of small waterfalls links the pools in a natural watery stairway from the mountain to the sea.

Upcountry Maui, home to proud *paniolos,* or Hawaiian cowboys, has the feel of Montana with a tropical twist.

The Polynesian-style peaked-roof lines of the Sheraton Maui grace the shore of the west-facing beach at Kā'anapali.

Storm-fed waterfalls pound into hidden plunge pools along the windward cliffs of Haleakalā between Kīpahulu and Kaupō.

A golden sunrise outlines the ragged contours of 'Ālau Island off the coast of Hāna.

Whales put Maui on the map 150 years ago, when whalers from the eastern U.S. and Europe used the safe and convenient anchorage at Lahaina for a central provisioning stop in the whale-rich northern Pacific. As many as 400 ships dropped anchor there every year during the 1840s. Grog shops and lawlessness proliferated, along with commerce and growth. At the time, Lahaina's native and foreign population was about 3,500 people and 528 dogs.

The discovery of petroleum in Pennsylvania in 1871 put an abrupt end to the whale oil business and the whaling fleets. The royal seat of the kingdom was moved to the larger commercial port at Honolulu on O'ahu. Lahaina was all but deserted.

For the next century, Maui slumbered as its vast lands were consolidated into sugar cane and pineapple plantations, and its mountain streams were tapped for irrigation water. Until the early 1960s, Maui was little more than a few plantation camps, cattle ranches, isolated fishing villages, a half-dozen Spartan hotels, and plenty of space. The sugar fields spread uninterrupted like rich lawns from the foot of the mountains to the beaches.

The public beach park at Fleming Beach was named for David Thomas Fleming, the early manager of Honolua Ranch and Baldwin Packers.

For 200 years of island history Lahaina Harbor was a major port and royal playground. Today, the harbor is home to fishing, tour, and pleasure boats that continue the rich tradition.

The tourist boom began at Kā'anapali in 1962. For the next 25 years and continuing today, resort hotels, golf courses, and vacation condominiums have seemed to sprout wherever there is a sunny swimming beach. Little Kahului airport, long accustomed to a few interisland flights daily, found itself welcoming nonstop jumbo jets direct from mainland U.S. cities.

At the same time, mainland hippies found the deeper meaning of "mellow" on Maui's remote beaches and in the smoky haze of its famous *pakalolo* (marijuana). The island became a world-renowned playground for the Age of Aquarius.

The current Maui lifestyle now attracts large numbers of "life-stylists" to the island's seaside condominiums and chic Upcountry cabins. These folk settle down for a few years as realtors, hotel bartenders, carpenters, small shop owners, and trust-fund windsurfers. As a result, Maui is the fastest growing and most heavily *haole* (Caucasian) of all the islands.

About two-and-a-half million visitors now spend $1.5 billion on Maui each year. On an average day, 42,000 visitors share the island with a resident population that has passed the 100,000 mark. Locals grumble about traffic that most newcomers barely notice.

Amid all the glitzy resorts and swank restaurants, Maui manages to keep its island character and its soaring beauty alive. To be enjoyed are its natural and man-made wonders, its country roads, ancient temples, peaceful beaches, blazing sunsets, misty rains, friendly smiles, and dewy flowers.

The roaring surf and sandy, white beach of Nāpili Bay, near Kīpahulu, make this a popular swimming spot for visitors and locals.

The resorts at Wailea, on the sunny southwest side of Haleakalā, offer grand hotels, condominiums, and world-class golf courses.

'Īao Needle, located in the West Maui Mountains, was the site where Kamehameha the Great defeated the armies of Maui's chief Kalanikupule.

Wailua Falls, on the Hāna Highway just before the Seven Pools of Kīpahulu, is an archetypal vision of paradise.

Once hunted in Hawai'i's coastal waters, the gentle humpback whales now breach and play with their new-born calves in the 'Au'au Channel off Lahaina.

At Kapalua the paved Honoapi'ilani Highway ends. Offshore, silhouetted by the setting sun, is the island of Moloka'i.

The broad white sand and glistening blue water of Mākena Beach in South Maui make this a local favorite.

Maui's unique wind and sea conditions are perfect for the sport of windsurfing.

The half-submerged crater, Molokini Islet, is a major feature of South Maui.

The stunning green ridges and dramatic cliffs of the northern coast of Moloka'i catch the trade wind rains and selfishly hoard the cool water. Shaped like the *mano* (shark), this island is home to Hawai'i's most culturally-connected Hawaiians.

FACTS
AND FIGURES
KAHO'OLAWE

Land area: Kaho'olawe, 44.6 square miles
Population: uninhabited
Highest point: Pu'u Moaulanui, 1,483 feet
Extreme length and width:
  11 miles by 6 miles

LĀNA'I

Land area: Lāna'i, 140.5 square miles
Population: 3,193 (2000)
Highest point: Lānaihale, 3,366 feet
Extreme length and width:
  18 miles by 13 miles
Hotel and condominium rental units: 367
  (2006)
Visitors per year: 105,575 (2006)

MOLOKA'I

Land area: Moloka'i, 260 square miles;
Population: 7,404 (2000)
Highest point: Kamakou, 4,961 feet
Extreme length and width:
  38 miles by 10 miles
Visitors per year: 95,510 (2006)

KAHO'OLAWE

Sheltered by the vast bulk of nearby Haleakalā from Hawai'i's moisture-laden northeast trade winds, low-lying Kaho'olawe is now barren red "hardpan," impenetrable to rain or roots. Kaho'olawe translates as "the carrying away," and the island has indeed been carried away in a 200-year plume of fine red dust.

Inhabited only intermittently in ancient times by fishermen, star-wise navigators, and gatherers of fine-grained basalt and obsidian (for spear points), Kaho'olawe enjoyed a brief commercial career in the 1930s as an offshore annex to Maui's Haleakalā and 'Ulupalakua ranches. But with the approach of World War II, civilian access was curtailed, and from 1940 to 1995 the island absorbed millions of rounds of U.S. and Allied naval and aircraft gunfire. It had become a target island for war games. Hawaiian activists succeeded in getting the Navy to give Kaho'olawe back to the state as a cultural sanctuary, but only after decades of dramatic protests.

While it has rarely been prominent commercially, Kaho'olawe often has been useful. Pre-Cook navigators supposedly used the island landmarks as guides for starting the long voyage back to Tahiti, and nineteenth century opium runners found the deserted island handy. Their legacy today is a sandy "Smugglers' Cove."

Opposite page: **The tiny island of Kaho'olawe, a desert environ trapped in the rainshadow of Maui's Haleakalā, once served as the ancient Hawaiian navigational landmark at the open-ocean entry to the island chain. In the post World War II years this 11-mile-long remnant of an old volcano was used as a bombing target by the United States Navy.**

Today, Kaho'olawe's virgin coves and reefs are a favorite landing point for pleasure cruises and snorkeling expeditions launched from the Maui ports of Lahaina and Māʻalaea.

Shipwreck Beach, a long stretch of wind-blown white sand on the north coast of Lāna'i, acquired its name during the late 1800s and early 1900s, when wooden sailing ships and steamers ran aground on the offshore reefs.

LĀNAʻI

One of the two "dry" islands lying in the rain shadow of Maui's immense Haleakalā (uninhabited Kahoʻolawe is the other), Lānaʻi attracted few settlements in ancient times. Wary of the ʻuhane (ghosts) and akua (fierce gods) which dwelt there, sensible Hawaiians avoided arid Lānaʻi for cooler, more moist Maui, Molokaʻi, and Oʻahu.

Pineapple planter James Dole laid the foundation for today's Lānaʻi when he plowed his first pineapple fields at Wahiawā, outside Honolulu, in 1901 and founded Hawaiʻi's first successful canning operation. Subsequently, his Dole Corporation purchased 98 percent of Lānaʻi island from the Territorial government. The remaining two percent is in pie-shaped land divisions owned by long-time Hawaiian families.

With a population of 2,400, largely descendants of Filipino, Portuguese, and Japanese immigrant workers, Lānaʻi City, the lone community, remains the state's foremost "company town," although many families long ago bought their own homes and businesses from Castle & Cooke, corporate owners of Dole. Until very recently, the community of lofty pines and tidy cottages was so quiet you could trace the progress of a jeep or pickup through Lānaʻi City by the sequential barking of dogs. But the late eighties brought changes when the pineapple plantation closed and two world-class resorts opened, one upland in Kōʻele, and the other at Mānele Bay.

Like their neighbors across the channel on Molokaʻi, Lānaʻi folks are known for their hunting and fishing skills, their self-sufficiency, their generosity, and their love of family and community. The island is famed for its forested uplands, empty wind-swept beaches, and the stark sea cliffs along the western shore, at the foot of which are some of Hawaiʻi's best fishing and diving.

The Kō'ele Lodge, one of Lāna'i's exclusive resorts, is nestled on an upland plateau that was once covered with a patchwork of pineapple fields.

The petroglyph field at Luahiwa is one of the sites where ancient Hawaiians left pictorial history etched into lava rock faces.

MOLOKA'I

Although its size and mountainous terrain would seemingly lump Moloka'i with the big islands of Hawai'i, Maui, O'ahu, and Kaua'i, the island's rural values and the survival skills of its residents bespeak a closer kinship with Lāna'i and Ni'ihau. With an economy that has been moribund for decades, Moloka'i produces more than its share of hunters, fishermen, and farmers.

It also has the state's most prominent ethnic Hawaiian community, due in part to the substantial Hawaiian Homestead acreage at Ho'olehua. Of Moloka'i's 7000 residents, about 5000 classify themselves as Hawaiian or part-Hawaiian, a ratio exceeded only on tiny Ni'ihau. Farming, fishing, and tourism are the principal dollar earners.

Two great ranches dominate the island—arid Moloka'i Ranch on the western half, and rainy Pu'u o Hoku ("hill of stars") Ranch in the east. In between are mile-high mountains, vast inaccessible valleys, and some of Hawai'i's broadest reefs. Locked up for years by Moloka'i Ranch, the splendid coves and beaches of Moloka'i's West End were finally opened to the public late in the 1970s, with the development of the Kaluako'i Resort near three-mile-long Pāpōhaku Beach.

On the island's wild and spectacular north shore opposite Kaunakakai is the famous Kalaupapa settlement where Father Damien de Veuster spent his last years administering to Hawai'i's neglected nineteenth century leprosy patients. Situated on a low peninsula guarded by some of the world's loftiest sea cliffs, Kalaupapa is a unique and soul-stirring community.

Opposite page: **Kalaupapa Peninsula was formed by a small shield volcano whose lava flow fanned into a flat, leaf-shaped land mass near the center of the northern coast of Moloka'i. During the leprosy epidemic of the mid-to-late 1800s, many of Hawai'i's Oriental and Hawaiian community were quarantined on this spit of isolated land. Today, the Kalaupapa settlement is designated as a National Park. The only land access to the park is down the 26 winding switch-backs along the cliff-side trail that has always served as Kalaupapa's link with the outside world.**

Hawai'i's nearly extinct flora is protected at the Kamakou Preserve near the peak of Moloka'i's east volcano.

Constructed in 1873, St. Philomena Church has come to represent Father Joseph Damien de Veuster's humanitarian work with the leper patients of Kalaupapa.

Planted by King Kamehameha V in the 1860s, the Kapuāiwa Coconut Grove once covered ten acres and contained over 1,000 trees.

Moa'ula Falls tumbles through the lush green depths of Halawa Valley on the northeastern tip of island of Moloka'i.

The Sheraton-Moloka'i, one of the island's luxury resorts, is perched on the northwestern tip of Kepuhi Bay. On a clear night the lights of O'ahu can be seen from Kepuhi Beach.

Steep seacliffs, sand dunes, a freshwater pool, and a rugged beach make up the dramatic Mo'omomi Preserve on Moloka'i's northeastern shore.

For many years this string of patient mules was the only transportation to and from the isolated community of Kalaupapa. Laboriously, these plodding caravans transported cargo down the steep and winding cliff-trail to the leper colony below.

ABOUT THE
AUTHORS

Author and environmentalist Curt Sanburn grew up in Hawai'i before graduating from Yale University in 1978. As a freelance writer and editor, he helped shape several books in the "A Day in the Life Of..." series, as well as other major coffeetable books.

U'i and Steven Goldsberry began collaborating on a series of writing projects three years ago, after their children graduated from Kahuku High School. Both are accomplished writers who continue to work on numerous projects.

ABOUT THE
PHOTOGRAPHER

Douglas Peebles has been capturing Hawai'i's beauty ever since he arrived in the Islands in 1974. He is a world traveler who has photographed in 45 countries.